Born in 1973

by

Kerry Butters.

Born in 1973

Millennium: **2nd millennium**

Centuries: 19th century – **20th century** – 21st century

Decades: 1940s 1950s 1960s – **1970s** – 1980s 1990s 2000s

     1973 (MCMLXXIII) was a common year starting on Monday (dominical letter G) of the Gregorian calendar, the 1973rd year of the Common Era (CE) and *Anno Domini* (AD) designations, the 973rd year of the 2nd millennium, the 73rd year of the 20th century, and the 4th year of the 1970s decade.

Contents

Events

January

- January 1 –
  - The United Kingdom, the Republic of Ireland and Denmark enter the European Economic Community, which later becomes the European Union.
  - CBS sells the New York Yankees for $10 million to a 12-person syndicate led by George Steinbrenner (3.2 million dollars less than CBS bought the Yankees for).
- January 5 – American rock band Aerosmith releases their debut album.
- January 7 – Mark Essex kills 9 people at the Howard Johnson's hotel in downtown New Orleans.
- January 14 –
  - Elvis Presley's concert in Hawaii is the first worldwide telecast by an entertainer, that is watched by more people than watched the Apollo moon landings.
  - American football: The Miami Dolphins complete the first (and through 2015, only) perfect season in National Football League history by defeating the Washington Redskins 14-7 in Super Bowl VII at the Los Angeles Memorial Coliseum.
- January 15 – Vietnam War: Citing progress in peace negotiations, U.S. President Richard Nixon announces the suspension of offensive action in North Vietnam.

- January 16 – Anna Christian Waters, 5 years old, disappears from her home in Purisima Canyon, near Half Moon Bay, California.
- January 17 – Ferdinand Marcos becomes President for Life of the Philippines.
- January 18 – Eleven Labour Party councillors in Clay Cross, Derbyshire, England, are ordered to pay £6,985 for not enforcing the Housing Finance Act.
- January 20 – U.S. President Richard Nixon is inaugurated for his second term.
- January 21 – The Communist League is founded in Denmark.
- January 22
  - *Roe v. Wade*: The U.S. Supreme Court overturns state bans on abortion.
  - George Foreman defeats Joe Frazier to win the heavyweight world boxing championship.
  - A Royal Jordanian Boeing 707 flight from Jeddah crashes in Kano, Nigeria; 176 people are killed.
  - Former U.S. President Lyndon B. Johnson dies at his Stonewall, Texas ranch, leaving no former U.S. President living until the resignation of Richard Nixon in 1974.
  - The crew of Apollo 17 addresses a joint session of Congress after the completion of the final Apollo moon landing mission.
- January 23
  - Eldfell on the Icelandic island of Heimaey erupts.
  - U.S. President Richard Nixon announces that a peace accord has been reached in Vietnam.
- January 25 – English actor Derren Nesbitt is convicted of assaulting his wife Anne Aubrey.
- January 27 – U.S. involvement in the Vietnam War ends with the signing of the Paris Peace Accords.
- January 31 – Pan American and Trans World Airlines cancelled their options to buy 13 Concorde airliners.

February

- February 6 – Toronto: Construction on the CN Tower begins.
- February 8 – A military insurrection in Uruguay poses an institutional challenge to President Juan María Bordaberry.
- February 11 – Vietnam War: The first American prisoners of war are released from Vietnam.
- February 12 – Ohio becomes the first U.S. state to post distance in metric on signs (see Metrication in the United States).
- February 13 – The United States dollar is devalued by 10%.
- February 16 – The Court of Appeal of England and Wales rules that *The Sunday Times* can publish articles on thalidomide and Distillers Company, despite ongoing legal actions by parents (the decision is overturned in July by the House of Lords).
- February 21 – Libyan Arab Airlines Flight 114 (Boeing 727) is shot down by Israeli fighter aircraft over the Sinai Desert, after the passenger plane is suspected of being an enemy military plane. Only 5 (1 crew member and 4 passengers) of 113 survive.
- February 22 – Sino-American relations: Following President Richard Nixon's visit to mainland China, the United States and the People's Republic of China agree to establish liaison offices.
- February 26 – Edward Heath's British government publishes a Green Paper on prices and incomes policy.

Flag of the American Indian Movement

- February 27 – The American Indian Movement occupies Wounded Knee, South Dakota.

- February 28
    - The Republic of Ireland general election is held. Liam Cosgrave becomes the new Taoiseach.
    - The landmark postmodern novel *Gravity's Rainbow* by Thomas Pynchon is published.

March

- March 1
    - *Charlotte's Web*, the animated movie based on the same name of the children's book is released.
    - Dick Taverne, having resigned from the Parliament of the United Kingdom on leaving the Labour Party, is re-elected as a 'Democratic Labour' candidate.
    - Pink Floyd's *The Dark Side of the Moon*, one of rock's landmark albums, is released in the US. It is released in the UK on March 24.
- March 2 – Wellington Street bus station in Perth, Australia, is opened by western Australia's premier John Tonkin
- March 3 – Tottenham Hotspur wins the Football League Cup final at Wembley, beating Norwich City 1–0.
- March 7 – Comet Kohoutek is discovered.
- March 8
    - Northern Ireland sovereignty referendum (the "Border Poll"): 98.9% of those voting in the province want Northern Ireland to remain within the United Kingdom. Turnout is 58.7%, although less than 1% for Catholics. This is the first referendum on regional government in the U.K.
    - Provisional Irish Republican Army bombs explode in Whitehall and the Old Bailey in London.
- March 10 – Sir Richard Sharples, Governor of Bermuda, is assassinated in Government House.
- March 12 – Last episode of original *Laugh-In* airs on NBC. The show will continue with re-runs until May 14, 1973.
-

- March 17
  - Elizabeth II opens the modern London Bridge.
  - Many of the few remaining United States soldiers begin to leave Vietnam. One reunion of a former POW with his family is immortalized in the Pulitzer Prize-winning photograph *Burst of Joy*.
- March 20 – A British government White Paper on Northern Ireland proposes the re-establishment of an Assembly elected by proportional representation, with a possible All-Ireland council.
- March 21 – The Lofthouse Colliery disaster occurs in Great Britain. Seven miners are trapped underground; none survive.
- March 23 – Watergate scandal (United States): In a letter to Judge John Sirica, Watergate burglar James W. McCord, Jr. admits that he and other defendants have been pressured to remain silent about the case. He names former Attorney General John Mitchell as 'overall boss' of the operation.
- March 26 – TV soap opera *The Young and the Restless* debuts on CBS.
- March 27 – At the 45th Academy Awards, *The Godfather* wins best picture.
- March 29 – The last United States soldier leaves Vietnam.

April

- April 2 – The LexisNexis computerized legal research service begins.
- April 3 – The first handheld mobile phone call is made by Martin Cooper of Motorola in New York City.
- April 4 – The World Trade Center officially opens in New York City with a ribbon-cutting ceremony.

- April 5

The launch of the Atlas-Centaur carrying the Pioneer G (11) spacecraft on April 5, 1973.

  - Fahri Korutürk becomes the sixth president of Turkey.
  - *Pioneer 11* is launched on a mission to study the Solar System.
- April 6 – Ron Blomberg of the New York Yankees becomes the first designated hitter in Major League Baseball.
- April 7 – *Tu te reconnaîtras* by Anne-Marie David (music by Claude Morgan, text by Vline Buggy) wins the Eurovision Song Contest 1973 for Luxembourg.
- April 8 – Artist Pablo Picasso dies at his home in France.
- April 10 – Israeli commandos raid Beirut, assassinating 3 leaders of the Palestinian Resistance Movement. The Lebanese army's inaction brings the immediate resignation of Prime Minister Saib Salam, a Sunni Muslim.
- April 11 – The British House of Commons votes against restoring capital punishment by a margin of 142 votes.
- April 12 – The Labour Party wins control of the Greater London Council.
- April 15 – Naim Talu, a former civil servant, forms the new government of Turkey (36th government).
- April 17
  - The German counter-terrorist force GSG 9 is officially formed in response to the Munich massacre.
  - Federal Express officially begins operations, with the launch of 14 small aircraft from Memphis International Airport. On

that night, Federal Express delivers 186 packages to 25 U.S. cities from Rochester, New York, to Miami, Florida.
- The Morganza Spillway on the Mississippi River is opened for the first time in order to prevent catastrophic flooding of New Orleans.
- April 20 – An Indian Pacific train en route to Perth derails near Broken Hill, New South Wales, destroying a quarter mile of track.
- April 26 – The first day of trading on the Chicago Board Options Exchange.
- April 28
  - The last section of the IRT Third Avenue Line from 149th Street to Gun Hill Road in The Bronx is closed.
  - Six Irishmen, including Joe Cahill, are arrested by the Irish Naval Service off County Waterford, on board a coaster carrying 5 tons of weapons destined for the Provisional Irish Republican Army.
- April 30 – Watergate scandal: President Richard Nixon announces that White House Counsel John Dean has been fired and that Attorney General Richard Kleindienst has resigned along with staffers H. R. Haldeman and John Ehrlichman.

May

- May 1 – An estimated 1,600,000 workers in the United Kingdom stop work in support of a Trades Union Congress "day of national protest and stoppage" against the Government's anti-inflation policy.

Sears Tower

- May 3 – The Sears Tower in Chicago is finished, becoming the world's tallest building at 1,451 feet.
- May 5
  - Shambu Tamang becomes the youngest person to climb to the summit of Mount Everest.
  - Sunderland A.F.C. defeats Leeds United A.F.C. in the 1973 FA Cup Final.
  - Secretariat wins the Kentucky Derby in a dramatic come from behind victory and setting a new Derby record of 1:59 2/5ths.
  - Led Zeppelin plays before 56,800 persons at Tampa Stadium on the band's 1973 North American Tour, thus breaking the August 15, 1965 record of 55,600 set by The Beatles at Shea Stadium.
- May 8 – A 71-day standoff between federal authorities and American Indian Movement activists who were occupying the Pine Ridge Reservation at Wounded Knee, South Dakota, ends with the surrender of the militants.

- May 10
  - The Montreal Canadiens win the Stanley Cup 4 games to 2 over the Chicago Blackhawks, Yvan Cournoyer was voted MVP.
  - The Polisario Front, a Sahrawi movement dedicated to the independence of Spanish Sahara, is formed.
  - The New York Knicks defeat the Los Angeles Lakers, 102–93 in Game 5 of the NBA Finals to win the NBA title.
- May 13
  - Bobby Riggs challenges and defeats Margaret Court, the world's #1 women's player, in a nationally-televised tennis match set in Ramona, CA northeast of San Diego. Riggs wins 6-2, 6-1 which leads to the huge Battle of the Sexes match against Billie Jean King later in the year on September 20.
- May 14
  - *Skylab*, the United States' first space station, is launched.
  - The British House of Commons votes to abolish capital punishment in Northern Ireland.
- May 17 – Watergate scandal: Televised hearings begin in the United States Senate.
- May 18 – Second Cod War: Joseph Godber, British Minister of Agriculture, Fisheries and Food, announces that Royal Navy frigates will protect British trawlers fishing in the disputed 50-mile limit round Iceland.
- May 19 – Secretariat wins the Preakness Stakes by 2 1/2 lengths over the amazingly quick 2nd placed Sham. A malfunction in the track's timing equipment prevented a confirmed new track record.
- May 22 – Lord Lambton resigns from the British government over a 'call girl' scandal.
- May 23 – Royal Canadian Mounted Police celebrate 100 year anniversary.
- May 24 – Earl Jellicoe, Lord Privy Seal and Leader of the House of Lords in Britain, resigns over a separate prostitution scandal.

- May 25
  - *Skylab 2* (Pete Conrad, Paul Weitz, Joseph Kerwin) is launched on a mission to repair damage to the recently launched *Skylab* space station.
  - Héctor José Cámpora becomes democratic president of the Argentine Republic ending the 1966 to 1973 Revolución Argentina military dictatorship.
- May 27 – By virtue of the non-retroactivity of Soviet copyright laws, all works published before this date are public domain. This applies worldwide.
- May 30–Gordon Johncock wins the Indianapolis 500 in the *Patrick Racing Special* Eagle-Offenhauser, after only 133 laps, due to rain. (The race was begun May 28 but called due to rain.)

June

- June 1 – The Greek military junta abolishes the monarchy and proclaims a republic.
- June 3 – A Tupolev Tu-144 crashes at the Paris air show; 15 are killed.
- June 4 – A patent for the ATM is granted to Donald Wetzel, Tom Barnes and George Chastain.
- June 9 – Secretariat wins the Belmont Stakes shattering the record by an unbelievable 2 3/5ths seconds, becoming the first Triple Crown of Thoroughbred Racing winner since 1948.
- June 10
  - Henri Pescarolo and co-driver Gérard Larrousse (both France) win the 24 Hours of Le Mans in the *Equipe Matra* MS670B.
  - The grandson of J. Paul Getty is kidnapped in Rome.
- June 16 – U.S. President Richard Nixon begins several talks with Soviet leader Leonid Brezhnev.
- June 17 – The submersible *Johnson Sea Link* becomes entangled on the wreckage of the USS *Fred T. Berry* off Key West, Florida.

The submersible is brought to the surface the following day, but 2 of the 4 men aboard die of carbon dioxide poisoning.

- June 20 – The Ezeiza massacre occurs in Buenos Aires, Argentina. Snipers shoot at left-wing Peronists, killing at least 13 and injuring more than 300.
- June 22 – W. Mark Felt ("Deep Throat") retires from the Federal Bureau of Investigation.
- June 23 – A house fire in Kingston upon Hull, England, which kills a 6-year-old boy is passed off as an accident; it later emerges as the first of 26 fire deaths caused over the next 7 years by arsonist Peter Dinsdale.
- June 24 – Soviet leader Leonid Brezhnev addresses the American people on television, the first to do so.
- June 25
  - Conference on Security and Cooperation in Europe (CSCE).
  - Erskine Hamilton Childers is elected the 4th President of Ireland.
  - Watergate scandal: Former White House counsel John Dean begins his testimony before the Senate Watergate Committee.
- June 26 – At Plesetsk Cosmodrome, 9 persons are killed in the explosion of a Cosmos 3-M rocket.
- June 27 – Coup d'état in Uruguay: pressed by the military, President Juan María Bordaberry dissolves Parliament; a 12-year-long civic-military dictatorship begins.
- June 28 – Elections are held for the Northern Ireland Assembly, which will lead to power-sharing between unionists and nationalists in Northern Ireland for the first time.
- June 30 – A very long total solar eclipse occurs. During the entire 2nd millennium, only 7 total solar eclipses exceeded 7 minutes of totality.

July

- July 1 – The United States Drug Enforcement Administration is founded.

- July 2 – The United States Congress passes the Education of the Handicapped Act (EHA) mandating Special Education federally.
- July 4 – MLB: The New York Mets fall 12½ games back in last place of the National League Eastern Division.
- July 5
  - The Isle of Man Post begins to issue its own postage stamps.
  - The catastrophic BLEVE (Boiling Liquid Expanding Vapor Explosion) occurs in Kingman, Arizona, following a fire that broke out as propane was being transferred from a railroad car to a storage tank, killing 11 firefighters. This explosion becomes a classic incident, studied in fire department training programs worldwide.

Saint Andrew's Cathedral, Singapore

- July 6 – St Andrew's Cathedral, Singapore is gazetted as a national monument.
- July 10 – The Bahamas gains full independence within the Commonwealth of Nations.
- July 11 – Varig Flight 820 crashes near Orly, France; 123 are killed.
- July 12 – National Personnel Records Center fire: A major fire destroys the entire 6th floor of the National Personnel Records Center in St. Louis, Missouri.
- July 16 – Watergate scandal: Former White House aide Alexander Butterfield informs the United States Senate Watergate Committee that President Richard Nixon had secretly recorded potentially incriminating conversations.

- July 17 – King Mohammed Zahir Shah of Afghanistan is deposed by his cousin Mohammed Daoud Khan while in Italy undergoing eye surgery.
- July 20 –
  - France resumes nuclear bomb tests in Mururoa Atoll, over the protests of Australia and New Zealand.
  - Bruce Lee, American actor, philosopher, founder of Jeet Kune Do, dies in Hong Kong of cerebral edema (six days later his final film, *Enter the Dragon*, is released).
- July 23 – The Avianca Building in Bogotá, Colombia suffers a serious fire.
- July 25 – The Soviet *Mars 5* space probe is launched.
- July 27 – The New York Dolls release their debut album.
- July 28
  - The Summer Jam at Watkins Glen, a massive rock festival featuring the Grateful Dead, The Allman Brothers Band and The Band, attracts over 600,000 music fans.
  - *Skylab 3* (Owen Garriott, Jack Lousma, Alan Bean) is launched, to conduct various medical and scientific experiments aboard *Skylab*.
- July 29 – Formula One racing driver Roger Williamson dies in an accident, witnessed live on European television, during the 1973 Dutch Grand Prix.
- July 30 – An 11-year legal action for the victims of Thalidomide ends.
- July 31
  - Militant protesters led by Ian Paisley disrupt the first sitting of the Northern Ireland Assembly.
  - A Delta Air Lines DC-9 aircraft flying as Delta Air Lines Flight 173 lands short of Boston's Logan Airport runway in poor visibility, striking a sea wall about 165 feet (50 m) to the right of the runway centerline and about 3,000 feet (914 m) short. All 6 crew members and 83 passengers are killed, 1 of the passengers dying several months after the accident.

August

Flag of CARICOM

- August 1 – Caribbean Community and Common Market (CARICOM) inaugurated.
- August 2 – A flash fire kills 51 at the Summerland amusement centre at Douglas, Isle of Man.
- August 5 – Black September members open fire at the Athens airport; 3 are killed, 55 injured.
- August 8
  - South Korean politician Kim Dae-jung is kidnapped in Tokyo by the KCIA.
  - The death of Dean Corll leads to the discovery of the Houston Mass Murders: a minimum of 28 boys were killed by Corll and his two teenage accomplices.
- August 15 – The U.S. bombing of Cambodia ends, officially halting 12 years of combat activity in Southeast Asia according to the Case–Church Amendment-an act that prohibites military operations in Laos, Cambodia, and North and South Vietnam as a follow up of the Paris Peace Accords.
- August 23 – The Norrmalmstorg robbery occurs, famous for the origin of the term Stockholm syndrome.

September

- September 3 – The British Trades Union Congress expels 20 members for registering under the Industrial Relations Act 1971.

- September 9 – Jackie Stewart places fourth at the Italian *Grand Prix* at Monza, becoming World Drivers' Champion, in the Tyrrell 003-Cosworth.
- September 11
  - Chile's democratically elected government is overthrown in a military coup after serious instability. President Salvador Allende allegedly commits suicide during the coup in the presidential palace, and General Augusto Pinochet heads a U.S.-backed military junta that governs Chile for the next 16 years.
  - Art Garfunkel finally releases his solo debut album *Angel Clare*, 17 years after starting his career.
- September 15 – Gustaf VI Adolf of Sweden dies. His grandson, Carl XVI Gustaf, becomes king.
- September 18 – The two German Republics, the Federal Republic of Germany (West Germany) and the German Democratic Republic (East Germany), are admitted to the United Nations.
- September 20 – The *Battle of the Sexes*: Billie Jean King defeats Bobby Riggs in a televised tennis match, 6–4, 6–4, 6–3, at the Astrodome in Houston, Texas. With an attendance of 30,492, this remains the largest live audience ever to see a tennis match in US history. The global audience that viewed on television in 36 countries was estimated at 90 million.
- September 20 – Singer-songwriter Jim Croce dies following a gig at Northwestern State University in Natchitoches, Louisiana. Croce boarded a small chartered plane that crashed on takeoff. All six people aboard were killed.
- September 22 – Henry Kissinger, United States National Security Advisor, starts his term as United States Secretary of State.
- September 23 – The Oakland Raiders defeat the Miami Dolphins 12-7, ending the Dolphins' unbeaten streak at 18. It is the Miami Dolphins' first loss since January 16, 1972 in Super Bowl VI.
- September 27
  - Soviet space program: Soyuz 12, the first Soviet manned flight since the Soyuz 11 tragedy in 1971, is launched.

- Luís Cabral declares the independence of the Republic of Guinea-Bissau from the Estado Novo regime in Portugal. It is later granted in September 1974.
- September 28 – The ITT Building in New York City is bombed in protest at ITT's alleged involvement in the September 11, 1973 coup d'état in Chile.
- September 30 – Yankee Stadium, known as "The House That Ruth Built", closes for a two-year renovation at a cost of $160 million. The New York Yankees play all of their home games at Shea Stadium in 1974 and 1975.

October

October 20: Sydney Opera House is opened by Elizabeth II

- October 6
  - Yom Kippur War begins: The fourth and largest Arab–Israeli conflict begins, as Egyptian and Syrian forces attack Israeli forces in the Sinai Peninsula and Golan Heights on Yom Kippur.
  - French Formula One driver François Cevert is killed in the Tyrrell 003-Cosworth during the U.S. *Grand Prix*. Cevert's teammate, World Champion Jackie Stewart, announces his retirement after the event.
- October 8 – LBC Radio begins broadcasting on 97.3 FM in London.

- October 10
  - Spiro T. Agnew resigns as Vice President of the United States and then, in federal court in Baltimore, pleads no contest to charges of income tax evasion on $29,500 he received in 1967, while he was governor of Maryland. He is fined $10,000 and put on 3 years' probation.
- October 14 – Thai popular uprising Students revolt in Bangkok – In the Thammasat student uprising over 100,000 people protest in Thailand against the Thanom military government, 77 are killed and 857 are injured by soldiers, Thailand.
- October 15 – Typhoon Ruth crosses Luzon, Philippines, killing 27 people and causing $5 million in damage.
- October 17 – An OPEC oil embargo against several countries supporting Israel triggers the 1973 energy crisis.
- October 20
  - The Saturday Night Massacre: U.S. President Richard Nixon orders Attorney General Elliot Richardson to dismiss Watergate Special Prosecutor Archibald Cox. Richardson refuses and resigns, along with Deputy Attorney General William Ruckelshaus. Solicitor General Robert Bork, third in line at the Department of Justice, then fires Cox. The event raises calls for Nixon's impeachment.
  - The Sydney Opera House is opened by Elizabeth II after 14 years of construction work.

October 30: Bosphorus Bridge was opened by Turkish President Fahri Korutürk

- October 25 – The Yom Kippur War ends.
- October 26 – The United Nations recognizes the independence of Guinea-Bissau.

- October 27 – The Canon City meteorite, a 1.4 kilogram chondrite type meteorite, strikes Earth in Fremont County, Colorado.
- October 30 – The Bosphorus Bridge in Istanbul, Turkey is completed, connecting the continents of Europe and Asia over the Bosporus for the first time in history.
- October 31 – Mountjoy Prison helicopter escape: Three Provisional Irish Republican Army members escape from Mountjoy Prison, Dublin, Republic of Ireland after a hijacked helicopter lands in the exercise yard.

November

- November 1 – Watergate scandal: Acting Attorney General Robert Bork appoints Leon Jaworski as the new Watergate Special Prosecutor.

Mariner 10 Space probe, on U.S. Stamps, Space Exploration History, Issue of 1975

- November 3
  - Pan Am cargo flight 160, a Boeing 707-321C, crashes at Logan International Airport, Boston, killing 3 people.
  - Mariner program: NASA launches *Mariner 10* toward Mercury (on March 29, 1974 it becomes the first space probe to reach that planet).
- November 7 – The Congress of the United States overrides President Richard Nixon's veto of the War Powers Resolution, which limits presidential power to wage war without congressional approval.

- November 8 – Millennium '73, a festival hosted by Guru Maharaj Ji at the Astrodome, is called by supporters the "most significant event in human history".
- November 11 – Egypt and Israel sign a United States-sponsored cease-fire accord.
- November 14 – In the United Kingdom, Princess Anne marries Captain Mark Phillips in Westminster Abbey (they divorce in 1992).
- November 16
  - Skylab program: NASA launches *Skylab 4* (Gerald Carr, William Pogue, Edward Gibson) from Cape Canaveral, Florida on an 84-day mission.
  - U.S. President Richard Nixon signs the Trans-Alaska Pipeline Authorization Act into law, authorizing the construction of the Alaska Pipeline.
- November 17
  - Watergate scandal: In Orlando, Florida, U.S. President Richard Nixon tells 400 Associated Press managing editors "I am not a crook."
  - The Athens Polytechnic uprising occurs against the military regime in Athens, Greece.
- November 21 – U.S. President Richard Nixon's attorney, J. Fred Buzhardt, reveals the existence of an 18½-minute gap in one of the White House tape recordings related to Watergate.
- November 25 – Greek dictator George Papadopoulos is ousted in a military coup led by Brigadier General Dimitrios Ioannidis.
- November 27 – The United States Senate votes 92–3 to confirm Gerald Ford as Vice President of the United States.
- November 29 – 104 people are killed in a Taiyo department store fire in Kumamoto, Kyūshū, Japan.

December

- December – Chile breaks diplomatic contacts with Sweden.

- December 1 – Papua New Guinea gains self-government from Australia.
- December 3 – Pioneer program: *Pioneer 10* sends back the first close-up images of Jupiter.
- December 6 – The United States House of Representatives votes 387–35 to confirm Gerald Ford as Vice President of the United States; he is sworn in the same day.
- December 14 – Rhodesia executes two Blacks at Salisbury Central Prison for murder
- December 15 – Gay rights: The American Psychiatric Association removes homosexuality from its DSM-II.
- December 16 – O. J. Simpson of the Buffalo Bills became the first running back to rush for 2,000 yards in a pro football season.
- December 18 – The Islamic Development Bank is created as a specialized agency of the Organisation of the Islamic Conference (OIC) (effective 12 August 1974).
- December 19 – Namco releases *Mach Storm*, a planetarium-like flight simulator simulating a McDonnell Douglas F-4 Phantom II in which players can bomb rail yards, seaports, fuel tanks, power stations, supply depots, NVA and Viet Cong military camps, and airfields around Hanoi while fighting off enemy NVAF MiG-17s, MiG-21s, Shenyang J-5s, Shenyang J-6s, Mil Mi-8 gunships, Antonov An-2 biplanes, SA-2 surface-to-air missiles, and Soviet naval vessels in the Vietnam War during Operation Linebacker and the Christmas bombing of North Vietnam.
- December 20 – Spanish prime minister Luis Carrero Blanco is assassinated in Madrid by the separatist organization ETA.
- December 23 – OPEC doubles the price of crude oil.
- December 25 – Movie premier for The Sting starring Robert Redford and Paul Newman in Manhattan.
- December 28 – The Endangered Species Act is passed in the United States.
- December 30 – Terrorist Carlos fails in his attempt to assassinate British businessman Joseph Sieff.

- December 31 – In the United Kingdom, due to coal shortages caused by industrial action, the Three-Day Week electricity consumption reduction measure comes into force.

Date unknown

- ODECA functions are suspended.
- Economist E. F. Schumacher publishes his book *Small Is Beautiful*.
- The New York Bible Society International's New International Version of the New Testament translated into modern American English is published.
- The National House Building Council is formed in the United Kingdom.
- The COSC The Swiss Official Chronometer testing Institute is founded in Switzerland by 5 Watch Cantons & Federation of the Swiss Watch Industry.
- The title Queen of Australia is created by the Royal Style and Titles Act.
- A large Song dynasty trade ship of c. 1277 A.D. is dredged up from the waters near the southern coast of China with 12 compartments in its hull. It confirms the descriptions of bulkheaded hull compartments for junks in Zhu Yu's *Pingzhou Table Talks* of 1119.
- The Sentosa Musical Fountain opens alongside the Fountain Gardens in Sentosa, Singapore.
- 5 teams tie for the rugby championship: Wales, England, France, Ireland, and Scotland.
- Lite Beer is introduced in the U.S. by the Miller Brewing Company.

Births

January

Sean Paul

Portia de Rossi

- January 1
  - Danny Lloyd, American actor
  - Bryan Thao Worra, Lao writer
  - Jimi Mistry, English actor
- January 4 – Greg de Vries, Canadian ice hockey player
- January 5
  - Uday Chopra, Indian actor
- January 6 – Scott Ferguson, Canadian ice hockey player
- January 7 – Jonna Tervomaa, Finnish singer
- January 9 – Sean Paul, Jamaican singer
- January 12
  - Joseph M. Smith, American actor, writer and producer
  - Hande Yener, Turkish singer
- January 13
  - Nikolai Khabibulin, Russian hockey player
  - Gloria Yip, Hong Kong actress

- January 14 – Giancarlo Fisichella, Italian race car driver
  - Katie Griffin, Canadian actress and singer
- January 15
  - Tomáš Galásek, Czech football player
  - Essam El-Hadary, Egyptian goalkepper
  - Maksim Martynov, Russian engineer
- January 16
  - Josie Davis, American actress
  - Scott Greenall, musician, recording engineer, producer, and performance artist
- January 17 – Cuauhtémoc Blanco, Mexican football player
- January 18
  - Burnie Burns, American filmmaker
  - Crispian Mills, British musician (The Jeevas, Kula Shaker)
- January 19
  - Ann Kristin Aarønes, Norwegian footballer
  - Wang Junxia, Chinese long-distance runner
  - Karen Lancaume, French actress (d. 2005)
  - Antero Manninen, Finnish cellist
  - Yevgeny Sadovyi, Russian swimmer
  - Aaron Yonda, American YouTube celebrity
- January 21 – Chris Kilmore, American rock DJ (Incubus)
- January 22 – Abi Tucker, Australian actor and singer
- January 26 – Brendan Rodgers, Northern Irish football manager
- January 27 – Shadmchr Aghili, Iranian pop singer, musician and composer
- January 29 – Louise Hindsgavl, Danish artist
  - Jason Schmidt, American baseball player
- January 30 – Jalen Rose, American basketball player
- January 31
  - Shingo Katayama, Japanese golfer
  - Portia de Rossi, American actress

February

Oscar De La Hoya

Mishal Husain

Tara Strong

ATB

Alexei Kovalev

- February 1
  - Yuri Landman, Dutch artist and musician
  - Nick Mitchell, American wrestler
  - Makiko Ohmoto, Japanese voice actress
  - Óscar Pérez Rojas, Mexican football goalkeeper
- February 2 – Aleksander Tammert, Estonian discus thrower
- February 3 – Ilana Sod, Mexican journalist
- February 4
  - James Hird, Australian rules footballer
  - Brett Hestla, American musician and record producer.
  - Oscar De La Hoya, American boxer
- February 5
  - Trijntje Oosterhuis, Dutch pop singer
  - Deng Yaping, Chinese table tennis player
- February 7
  - Turki Al-Dakhil, Saudi journalist
  - Juwan Howard, American retired professional basketball player
  - Angel Aquino, Filipina model, actress and host
  - Mie Sonozaki, Japanese voice actress
  - Kate Thornton, British television presenter
- February 8 – Sonia Deol, British-Asian presenter
- February 9 – Svetlana Boginskaya, Soviet gymnast
- February 10
  - Gunn-Rita Dahle, Norwegian mountain biker
  - Núria Añó, Spanish writer
  -

- February 11
  - Jeon Do-yeon, South Korean actress
  - Mishal Husain, British news presenter for the BBC
  - Craig Jones, American rock sampler (Slipknot)
  - Varg Vikernes, Norwegian rock musician (Burzum)
- February 12 – Tara Strong, Canadian-born voice actress
- February 14 – Steve McNair, American football player (d. 2009)
- February 15 – Amy Van Dyken, American swimmer
- February 16 – Cathy Freeman, Australian athlete
- February 18 – Claude Makélélé, French footballer
- February 20 – Kimberley Davies, Australian actress
- February 21 – Heri Joensen, Faroese musician (Týr)
- February 22
  - Shota Arveladze, Georgian football player
  - Gustavo Assis-Brasil, Brazilian guitarist
  - Scott Phillips, American rock drummer
- February 24
  - Alexei Kovalev, Russian ice hockey player
  - Yordan Yovchev, Bulgarian gymnast
- February 26
  - ATB, German DJ and music producer
  - Anders and Jonas Björler, guitarists
  - Marshall Faulk, American football player
  - Ole Gunnar Solskjær, Norwegian footballer
  - Jenny Thompson, American swimmer
- February 27 – Peter Andre, English singer and television personality
- February 28
  - Eric Lindros, Canadian hockey player
  - Masato Tanaka, Japanese professional wrestler

March

Jim Parsons

Larry Page

Adam Goldstein

- March 1
  - Jack Davenport, English actor
  - Anton Gunn, American politician
  - Ahmed El Sakka, Egyptian action actor
  - Kathrine Lee-Hinton, American flight attendant
  - Chris Webber, American basketball player

- March 3 – Dejan Bodiroga, Serbian basketball player
- March 4 – Jennifer Cole, American actress, model and game show hostess
- March 5 – Ryan Franklin, American baseball pitcher
- March 6
    - Peter Lindgren, Swedish musician
    - Rumi Ochiai, Japanese voice actress
- March 7 – Rick Emerson, American talk show host and author
- March 9 – Aaron Boone, American baseball player
- March 10
    - Eva Herzigová, Czech model and actress
    - John LeCompt, American musician
    - Dan Swanö, Swedish musician
- March 13
    - Edgar Davids, Dutch footballer
    - David Draiman songwriter and lead singer for the band Disturbed
    - Ólafur Darri Ólafsson, Icelandic actor
- March 15 – Lee Jung-jae, South Korean actor and model
- March 17 – Caroline Corr, Irish musician (The Corrs)
- March 18 – Luci Christian, American voice actress
- March 19
    - Magnus Hedman, Swedish footballer
    - Simmone Jade Mackinnon, Australian actor
- March 20 – Arjun Atwal, Indian golfer
- March 23 – Jason Kidd, American basketball player
- March 24
    - Jacek Bąk, Polish footballer
    - Jim Parsons, American actor and comedian
- March 25 – Anders Fridén, Swedish musician
- March 26
    - T. R. Knight, American actor
    - Larry Page, American entrepreneur, founder of and former CEO of Google (2011-2015)
- March 27 – Sayaka Aoki, Japanese comedian
-

- March 28
  - Matt Nathanson, American singer-songwriter
  - Umaga, American wrestler (d. 2009)
- March 29 – Marc Overmars, Dutch footballer
- March 30 – Adam Goldstein, American DJ (d. 2009)

April

Pharrell Williams

Christian O'Connell

Adrien Brody

Lee Westwood

- April 1
  - Stephen Fleming, New Zealand cricket captain
  - Rachel Maddow, American political commentator
  - Kris Marshall, British actor
- April 2 – Roselyn Sánchez, Puerto Rican-American actress
- April 3
  - Jamie Bamber, English actor
  - Matthew Ferguson, Canadian actor
- April 4
  - David Blaine, American magician
  - Loris Capirossi, Italian motorcycle racer
- April 5
  - Élodie Bouchez, French actress
  - Cho Sung-min, South Korean baseball pitcher (d. 2013)
  - Pharrell Williams, American musician and producer (The Neptunes)
- April 6
  - Rie Miyazawa, Japanese actress and singer
  - Lori Heuring, American actress
- April 7 – Christian O'Connell, British radio DJ and presenter
- April 8 – Emma Caulfield, American actress
- April 10 – Roberto Carlos, Brazilian footballer
- April 11 – Jennifer Esposito, American actress
- April 12 – Amr Waked, Egyptian film, television, and stage actor
- April 13 – Sergey Shnurov, Russian singer

- April 14 – Adrien Brody, Academy Award-winning American actor
- April 15 – Emanuel Rego, Brazilian beach volleyball player
- April 16 – Akon, Senegalese American rapper, R&B singer, songwriter, and record producer
- April 18 – Haile Gebrselassie, Ethiopian long-distance runner
- April 19 – George Gregan, Australian rugby union footballer
- April 21
  - Mark Dexter, British actor
  - Katsuyuki Konishi, Japanese voice actor
- April 22 – Christopher Sabat, American voice actor
- April 24
  - Sachin Tendulkar, Indian cricketer
  - Lee Westwood, English golfer
- April 25 – Fredrik Larzon, Swedish rock musician (Millencolin)
- April 27 – Sharlee D'Angelo, Swedish guitarist
- April 28
  - Melissa Fahn, American actress
  - Elisabeth Röhm, German-American actress
- April 29 – David Belle, French actor
- April 30 – Jeff Timmons, American singer

May

Tori Spelling

Ruslana

Demetri Martin

- May 1
  - Paul Burke, Irish rugby player
  - Diana Hayden, former Miss World and Indian actress
  - Oliver Neuville, German footballer
- May 2 – Florian Henckel von Donnersmarck, German director
- May 3
  - Brad Martin, American musician
  - Michael Reiziger, Dutch footballer
- May 4 – Guillermo Barros Schelotto, Argentine footballer
- May 7 – Paolo Savoldelli, Italian professional road racing cyclist
- May 8
  - Hiromu Arakawa, Japanese manga artist
  - Marcus Brigstocke, British comedian
- May 9 – Tegla Loroupe, Kenyan long-distance runner
- May 10
  - Gareth Ainsworth, English footballer
  - Rüştü Reçber, Turkish football goalkeeper
- May 12
  - Forbes March, American actor
  - Robert Tinkler, Canadian voice actor
- May 14
  - Natalie Appleton, Canadian singer (All Saints)
  - Shanice, African-American singer

- May 16
  - Jason Acuña, American skateboarder and actor
  - Tori Spelling, American actress
  - Kōsuke Toriumi, Japanese voice actor
  - Muna AbuSulayman, Influential Arab and Muslim Media personality
- May 17
  - Sasha Alexander, American actress
  - Joshua Homme, American musician
  - Tamsier Joof, British dancer, choreographer and entrepreneur (of Senegalese and Gambian descent)
- May 18 – Kaz Hayashi, Japanese professional wrestler
- May 19 – Dario Franchitti, former Scottish racecar driver
- May 20 – Kaya Yanar, German comedian
- May 21 – Noel Fielding, British comedian
- May 23 – Jacopo Gianninoto, Italian musician
- May 24
  - Dermot O'Leary, British TV presenter
  - Ruslana, Ukrainian pop star, activist, Eurovision Song Contest 2004 winner
- May 25
  - Jean-Pierre Canlis, American glass artist
  - Demetri Martin, American comedian
- May 30 – Leigh Francis, British comedian
- May 31
  - Cadaveria, Italian singer (Opera IX)
  - Dominique van Roost, Belgian tennis player

June

Heidi Klum

Neil Patrick Harris

Carson Daly

Marie N

- June 1
    - Fred Deburghgraeve, Belgian swimmer
    - Adam Garcia, Australian actor and singer
    - Heidi Klum, German model
    - Derek Lowe, American baseball player
- June 2
    - Carlos Acosta, Cuban-born ballet dancer
    - Kevin Feige, American film producer and president of Marvel Studios
- June 8 – Lexa Doig, Canadian actress
- June 9 – Tedy Bruschi, American football player
- June 10 – Faith Evans, American singer
- June 12
    - Mitsuki Saiga, Japanese voice actress
    - Darryl White, Australian footballer
- June 13 – Sam Adams, American football player
- June 14 – Ceca Raznatovic, Serbian folk singer
- June 15
    - Dean McAmmond, Canadian hockey player
    - Neil Patrick Harris, American actor, singer, presenter, host
    - Greg Vaughan, American actor
- June 18 – Yumi Kakazu, Japanese voice actress
- June 19 – Yuko Nakazawa, Japanese singer
- June 20 – Chino Moreno, American musician
- June 21 – Juliette Lewis, American actress
- June 22 – Carson Daly, American television personality, host of *The Voice* and *Last Call with Carson Daly*
- June 23 – Marija Naumova (Marie N), Latvian singer, Eurovision Song Contest 2002 winner
- June 24 – Alexander Beyer, German actor
- June 25 – Jamie Redknapp, English footballer
- June 26 – Paweł Małaszyński, Polish actor
- June 27 – Olve Eikemo, Norwegian musician
- June 28 – Adrián Annus, Hungarian athlete
- June 30

- Robert Bales, United States Army staff-sergeant and suspect of the Kandahar massacre
- Chan Ho Park, Korean Major League Baseball player

July

Peter Kay

Peter Forsberg

Rufus Wainwright

Kate Beckinsale

- July 2 – Peter Kay, British comedian
- July 3 – Emma Cunniffe, British actress
- July 4 – Gackt, Japanese singer-songwriter and actor
- July 6 – Charizma, African-American rapper (d. 1993)
- July 7 – Natsuki Takaya, Japanese manga artist
- July 9 – Kelly Holcomb, American football player
- July 11 – Konstantinos Kenteris, Greek athlete
- July 12 – Christian Vieri, Italian footballer
- July 13 – Roberto Martínez, Spanish football manager
- July 14 – Halil Mutlu, Bulgaria-born Turkish weightlifter
- July 15
  - John Dolmayan, Lebanese-born rock drummer for the band System of a Down
  - Brian Austin Green, American actor
- July 16
  - Stefano Garzelli, Italian professional road racing cyclist
  - Graham Robertson, American filmmaker and author
- July 17
  - Eric Moulds, American football player
  - Liam Kyle Sullivan, American comedian
- July 19
  - Aílton Gonçalves da Silva, Brazilian football player
- July 20
  - Peter Forsberg, Swedish hockey player
  - HRH Crown Prince Haakon of Norway
- July 22
  - Daniel Jones, Australian musician and record producer
  - Rufus Wainwright, American-Canadian musician
- July 23
  - Omar Epps, American actor
  - Nomar Garciaparra, American baseball player
  - Fran Healy, Scottish singer-songwriter (Travis)
  - Monica Lewinsky, American former White House intern
- July 25
  - Kevin Phillips, English footballer
  - Tony Vincent, American actor and singer

- July 26 – Kate Beckinsale, English actress
- July 27 – Gorden Tallis, Australian rugby league player
- July 28 – Steve Staios, Canadian ice hockey player
- July 29 – Wanya Morris, African-American singer (Boyz II Men)
- July 30
  - Markus Näslund, Swedish ice hockey player
  - Sonu Nigam, Indian singer
- July 31 – Jacob Aagaard, Danish-Scottish chess player

August

Edurne Pasaban

Vera Farmiga

Kristen Wiig

Sergey Brin

- August 1 – Edurne Pasaban, Basque Spanish mountaineer
- August 2
  - Miguel Mendonca, Anglo-Azorean writer
  - Susie O'Neill, Australian swimmer
- August 6
  - Asia Carrera, American actress
  - Vera Farmiga, American actress
- August 8
  - Jessica Calvello, American voice actress
  - Scott Stapp, American singer and songwriter (Creed)
- August 9
  - Filippo Inzaghi, Italian footballer
  - Oleksandr Ponomariov, Ukrainian singer
- August 11 – Carolyn Murphy, American model
- August 12 – Richard Reid, English terrorist
- August 13 – Ryoko Shinohara, Japanese actress
- August 14
  - Jared Borgetti, Mexican footballer
  - Jay-Jay Okocha, Nigerian footballer
  - Kieren Perkins, Australian swimmer
- August 15 – Adnan Sami, music composer, pianist, singer
- August 16 – Damian Jackson, baseball player
- August 19
  - HRH Crown Princess Mette-Marit of Norway
  - Marco Materazzi, Italian football player
- August 20 – Todd Helton, American baseball player
-

- August 21
    - Sergey Brin, Russian-born American entrepreneur, co-founder of Google
    - Steve McKenna, hockey player
    - Nikolai Valuev, Russian heavyweight boxing champion
- August 22
    - Howie Dorough, American singer (Backstreet Boys)
    - Kristen Wiig, American actress and comedian
- August 24
    - Dave Brown, English comedian
    - Inge de Bruijn, Dutch swimmer
    - Dave Chappelle, African-American actor, comedian
    - Carmine Giovinazzo, American actor
    - Grey DeLisle, voice actress
- August 28 – Kirby Morrow, Canadian voice actor
- August 29 – Abdo Hakim, Lebanese actor and voice actor
- August 30 – Lisa Ling, American journalist

September

Andrew Lincoln

Nas

- September 1 – Ram Kapoor, Indian actor
- September 3 – Jennifer Paige, American singer-songwriter

- September 4
  - Jason David Frank, American actor and martial artist
  - Diosbelys Hurtado, Cuban boxer
- September 5 – Rose McGowan, American actress
- September 6
  - Carlo Cudicini, Italian footballer
  - Greg Rusedski, Canadian-British tennis player
- September 7 – Shannon Elizabeth, American actress
- September 9 – Kazuhisa Ishii, Japanese baseball player
- September 12
  - Darren Campbell, British athlete
  - Paul Walker, American actor (d. 2013)
- September 13 – Fabio Cannavaro, Italian footballer
- September 14
  - Andrew Lincoln, British actor
  - Nas, African-American rapper
- September 15
  - Indira Levak, Croatian lead vocalist of Colonia
  - Julie Cox, English actress
  - Prince Daniel, Duke of Västergötland, né Olof Daniel Westling, Swedish prince, married to Crown Princess Victoria
- September 17 – Ada Choi, Hong Kong actress
- September 18
  - Paul Brousseau, Canadian ice hockey player
  - James Marsden, American actor
  - Ami Onuki, Japanese singer
  - Mark Shuttleworth, South African entrepreneur
- September 19
  - José Azevedo, Portuguese cyclist
  - David Zepeda, Mexican actor, model and singer
- September 20 – Jo Pavey, British athlete
- September 21 – Oswaldo Sánchez, Mexican footballer
- September 22
  - Craig McRae, Australian footballer
  - Yoo Chae-yeong, South Korean singer and actress

- September 24 – Eddie George, American football player
- September 25 – Bridgette Wilson-Sampras, American actress
- September 26 – Lainey Lui, Canadian television personality; one of the co-hosts of etalk
- September 29
    - Alfie Boe, English tenor
    - Joe Hulbig, American ice hockey player

October

Mario López

Alex Tagliani

Seth MacFarlane

Adam Copeland

Verka Serduchka

Kari Korhonen (centre)

- October 1 – Christian Borle, American actor and singer
- October 2
  - Melissa Harris-Perry, African-American political commentator
  - Lene Nystrøm, Norwegian singer (Aqua)
  - Verka Serduchka, Ukrainian Drag queen, comedian and singer, Eurovision Song Contest 2007 runner-up
- October 3
  - Neve Campbell, Canadian actress
  - Richard Ian Cox, Welsh voice actor and radio host
- October 4
  - Chris Parks, American professional wrestler
  - Craig Robert Young, British actor and singer (Deuce)
- October 5 – Annabelle Chvostek, Canadian singer-songwriter
- October 6 – Ioan Gruffudd, Welsh actor
- October 8 – Kari Korhonen, Finnish cartoonist

- October 9
  - Steve Burns, *Blue's Clues* actor
  - Fabio Lione, Italian singer
- October 10 – Mario López, American actor
- October 11
  - Takeshi Kaneshiro, Taiwanese/Japanese actor
  - Daisuke Sakaguchi, Japanese voice actor
- October 13
  - Matt Hughes, American mixed martial arts fighter
  - Nanako Matsushima, Japanese actress
- October 14 – Lasha Zhvania, Georgian politician
- October 15
  - Susy Pryde, New Zealand cyclist
  - Dax Riggs, American musician
  - October 16, – Todd van der Heyden, Canadian journalist and news anchor
- October 18
  - Rachel Nichols, American sports journalist
  - Alex Tagliani, Canadian race car driver
- October 19 – Joaquin Gage, Canadian ice hockey player
- October 21 – Beverley Turner, British TV and radio presenter
- October 22 – Ichiro Suzuki, Japanese baseball player
- October 24 – Levi Leipheimer, American professional cyclist
- October 25
  - Lamont Bentley, American actor (d. 2005)
  - Maxi Mounds, American female stripper
- October 26
  - Seth MacFarlane, American animator and voice actor; creator of Family Guy and American Dad!
  - Taka Michinoku, Japanese professional wrestler
- October 28
  - Maryam Nawaz, Pakistani politician
  - Montel Vontavious Porter, WWE Raw wrestler
- October 29 – Robert Pirès, French football player

- October 30
  - Adam Copeland, retired Canadian professional wrestler and 4-time WWE Champion
  - Silvia Corzo, Colombian newsreader

November

Aishwarya Rai

Ryan Giggs

- November 1
  - Assia, Algerian singer
  - Li Xiaoshuang, Chinese gymnast
  - Aishwarya Rai, Indian actress, Miss World 1994
- November 3
  - Mick Thomson, American guitarist
  - Kirk Jones, African-American rapper (Onyx)
- November 5
  - Johnny Damon, baseball player
  - Peter Emmerich, American illustrator
- November 6 – Rumi Shishido, Japanese voice actress and singer
- November 8 – David Muir, American journalist and news anchor
-

- November 9
  - Alyson Court, Canadian actress
  - Nick Lachey, American singer
  - Maija Vilkkumaa, Finnish pop rock singer
- November 10
  - Jacqui Abbott, English singer
  - Róbert Gulya, Hungarian composer
- November 14
  - Lawyer Milloy, American football player
  - Dana Snyder, American voice actor
- November 19 – Billy Currington, American country singer
- November 20 – Sav Rocca, American football player and Australian rules footballer
- November 22 – Cassie Campbell, Canadian ice hockey forward and CBC commentator
- November 26 – Peter Facinelli, American actor
- November 27 – Sharlto Copley, South African producer, actor, and director
- November 28
  - Rob Conway, American professional wrestler
  - Jade Puget, American guitarist
  - Gina Tognoni, American actress
- November 29
  - Ryan Giggs, Welsh footballer
  - Raphael Smith, South African screenwriter and songwriter
- November 30
  - Nimród Antal, Hungarian-American film director, screenwriter and actor
  - Im Chang-jung, South Korean actor
  - Jason Reso, Canadian professional wrestler

December

Monica Seles

Tyra Banks

Stephenie Meyer

Seth Meyers

- December 2
  - Monica Seles, Hungarian-Yugoslavian tennis player
  - Jan Ullrich, German professional road bicycle racer
- December 3 – Holly Marie Combs, American actress
- December 4
  - Tyra Banks, American supermodel, talk show host
  - Steven Menzies, Australian rugby league player
  - Michael Jackson, former English football defender
- December 5
  - Mikelangelo Loconte, Italian singer
  - Neil Codling, Member of Suede
- December 7
  - Terrell Owens, American football player
  - Damien Rice, Irish singer-songwriter, musician and record producer
- December 8 – Corey Taylor, American rock vocalist (Slipknot, *Stone Sour)*
- December 9 – Bárbara Padilla American operatic soprano
- December 10 – Arden Myrin, American comedian
- December 11 – Mos Def, African-American rapper and actor
- December 14
  - Tomasz Radzinski, Canadian footballer
  - Thuy Trang, Vietnamese-born actress (d. 2001)
- December 15 – Surya Bonaly, French figure skater
- December 16 – Scott Storch, American hip-hop producer
- December 17 – Paula Radcliffe, British athlete

- December 18 – Darryl Brown, Trinidad and West Indian cricketer
- December 20 – Antti Kasvio, Finnish swimmer
- December 21 – Mike Alstott, American football player
- December 24
  - Paul Foot, English comedian
  - Stephenie Meyer, American novelist
  - Kerry Nettle, Australian politician
- December 25
  - Shalom Harlow, Canadian model and actress
  - Chris Harris, American professional wrestler
- December 27
  - Wilson Cruz, American actor
  - Kristoffer Zegers, Dutch composer
- December 28
  - Seth Meyers, American actor and comedian, currently hosts Late Night with Seth Meyers
  - Ids Postma, Dutch speed skater
- December 29
  - Theo Epstein, American baseball general manager
  - Pimp C, American rap artist
- December 30
  - Jason Behr, American actor
  - Ato Boldon, West Indian athlete
- December 31 – Nikolay Tsiskaridze, Russian dancer

Date unknown

- Tiago Carneiro da Cunha, Brazilian artist
- Eimear Quinn, Irish Celtic singer, Eurovision Song Contest 1996 winner

Deaths

January

Lyndon B. Johnson

- January 1
  - Sir Arthur Elton, pioneer of the British documentary film industry (b. 1906)
  - Sergei Kourdakov, former KGB agent (b. 1951)
- January 2 – Eleazar López Contreras, 32th President of Venezuela (b. 1883)
- January 7 – Mark Essex, American spree killer (b. 1949)
- January 8 – Dudley Foster, British actor (b. 1924)
- January 12 – Turk Edwards, American football player (Washington Redskins) and a member of the Pro Football Hall of Fame (b. 1907)
- January 17 – Herbert D. Riley, United States Navy admiral (b. 1904)
- January 19 – Max Adrian, Northern Irish actor (b. 1903)
- January 22 – Lyndon B. Johnson, 36th President of the United States (b. 1908)
- January 23 – Kid Ory, American musician (b. 1886)
- January 24 – J. Carrol Naish, American actor (b. 1897)
- January 26 – Edward G. Robinson, American actor (b. 1893)
- January 28 – John Banner, Austrian-born actor (b. 1910)
- January 29 – Ludwig Stössel, Austrian actor (b. 1883)

- January 31 – Ragnar Anton Kittil Frisch, Norwegian economist, Nobel Prize laureate (b. 1895)

February

Hans D Jensen

- February 11 – Hans D. Jensen, German physicist, Nobel Prize laureate (b. 1907)
- February 15
    - Wally Cox, American actor (b. 1924)
    - Tim Holt, American actor (b. 1919)
- February 16 – Francisco Caamaño, Dominican politician (b. 1932)
- February 17 – Harold Saxton Burr, American scientist (b. 1889)
- February 19 – Joseph Szigeti, Hungarian violinist (b. 1892)
- February 22
    - Elizabeth Bowen, Irish novelist (b. 1899)
    - Katina Paxinou, Greek actress (b. 1900)
- February 23 – Dickinson W. Richards, American physician, recipient of the Nobel Prize in Physiology or Medicine (b. 1895)
- February 28 – Cecil Kellaway, South African actor (b. 1893)

March

Pearl S. Buck

Ken Maynard

Noël Coward

- March 3 – Vera Panova, Soviet-Russian writer (b. 1905)
- March 4 – Marie-Anne Desmarest, French novelist (b. 1904)
- March 6 – Pearl S. Buck, American writer, Nobel Prize laureate (b. 1892)
- March 8 – Ron "Pigpen" McKernan, American rock musician (Grateful Dead) (b. 1945)
- March 10 – Bull Connor, Commissioner of Public Safety for the city of Birmingham, Alabama during the American Civil Rights Movement and member of the Ku Klux Klan during the 1920s (b. 1897)
- March 10 – Robert Siodmak, German-American director (b. 1900)
- March 12 – Frankie Frisch, American baseball player (St. Louis Cardinals) and a member of the MLB Hall of Fame (b. 1898)
- March 13 – Melville Cooper, British actor (b. 1896)
- March 14
  - Rafael Godoy, Colombian composer (b. 1907)
  - Chic Young, American cartoonist (b. 1901)
- March 18
  - Johannes Aavik, Estonian philologist (b. 1880)

- o Lauritz Melchior, Danish opera singer (b. 1890)
- March 20 – Adolf Strauss, German general (b. 1879)
- March 23 – Ken Maynard, American actor (b. 1895)
- March 25 – Edward Steichen, American photographer (b. 1879)
- March 26
  - o Safford Cape, American composer and musicologist (b. 1906)
  - o Sir Noël Coward, English composer and playwright (b. 1899)
  - o George Sisler, American baseball player (St. Louis Browns) and a member of the MLB Hall of Fame (b. 1893)
- March 30 – Douglas Douglas-Hamilton, 14th Duke of Hamilton, Scottish nobleman and pioneering aviator (b. 1903)

April

Xu Lai

Pablo Picasso

Arthur Fadden

- April 4 – Xu Lai, Chinese actress and secret agent (b. 1909)
- April 8 – Pablo Picasso, Spanish artist (b. 1881)
- April 12
  - Henry Darger, reclusive American outsider artist (b.1892)
  - Arthur Freed, American film producer (b. 1894)
- April 16
  - Nino Bravo, singer (b. 1944)
  - Istvan Kertesz, Hungarian conductor (b. 1929)
- April 19 – Hans Kelsen, Austrian-born legal theorist (b. 1881)
- April 20 – Robert Armstrong, American actor (b. 1890)
- April 21
  - Merian C. Cooper, American aviator, director, and producer (b. 1893)
  - Arthur Fadden, 13th Prime Minister of Australia (b. 1894)
- April 25
  - Armand Annet, French colonial official (b. 1888)
  - Frank Jack Fletcher, American admiral (b. 1885)
- April 26 – Irene Ryan, American actress (b. 1902)
- April 28 – Jacques Maritain, Catholic philosopher (b. 1882)
- April 30 – Václav Renč, Czech poet, dramatist and translator (b. 1911)

May

- May 1 – Asger Jorn, Danish painter (b. 1914)
- May 2 – Alan Carney, American actor and comedian (b. 1909)
- May 6 – Myrna Fahey, American actress (b. 1933)
- May 8 – Alexander Vandegrift, American general (b. 1887)
- May 10 – Jack E. Leonard, American comedian (b. 1910)
- May 11 – Lex Barker, American actor (b. 1919)
- May 12 – Frances Marion, American screenwriter (b. 1888)
- May 14 – Jean Gebser, German author, linguist, and poet (b. 1905)
- May 16 – Jacques Lipchitz, French American sculptor (b. 1891)
- May 18
  - Dieudonné Costes, French aviator (b. 1892)
  - Jeannette Rankin, first U.S. Congresswoman (b. 1880)

- May 20 – Jarno Saarinen, Finnish motorcycle racer (b. 1945)
- May 21
    - Ivan Konev, Marshal of the USSR (b. 1897)
    - Vaughn Monroe, American singer (b. 1911)
- May 26
    - Jay C. Higginbotham, American musician (b. 1906)
    - Karl Löwith, German philosopher (b. 1897)

June

- June 1 – Mary Kornman, American actress (b. 1915)
- June 3 – Dory Funk, American professional wrestler (b. 1919)
- June 4 – Arna Bontemps, African-American Harlem Renaissance writer (b. 1902)
- June 5 – Max Terhune, American actor (b. 1891)
- June 8 – Emmy Göring *nee* Sonnemann, German actress, second wife of Hermann Göring (b. 1893)
- June 9 – Erich von Manstein, German field marshal (b. 1887)
- June 10 – William Inge, American playwright (b. 1913)
- June 18 – Roger Delgado, English actor (b. 1918)
- June 23 – Fay Holden, American actress (b. 1893)
- June 24 – Mary Carr, American actress (b. 1874)
- June 26 – Ernest Truex, American actor (b. 1889)
- June 30
    - Nancy Mitford, English novelist (b. 1904)
    - Blessed Vasyl Velychkovsky C.Ss.R, Ukrainian Catholic bishop and martyr (b. 1903)

July

Betty Grable

Veronica Lake

Robert Ryan

Bruce Lee

Eddie Rickenbacker

- July 1 – Yosef Alon, Israeli pilot, co-founder of the Israeli Air Force, assassinated in the United States (b. 1929)
- July 2
    o Betty Grable, American actress (b. 1916)

- Chick Hafey, American baseball player (St. Louis Cardinals) and a member of the MLB Hall of Fame (b. 1903)
- George Macready, American actor (b. 1899)
- Swede Savage, American race car driver (b. 1946)
- July 5 – Golwalkar, Second sarsanghchalak of Rashtriya Swayamsevak Sangh (b. 1906)
- July 6
  - Joe E. Brown, American actor (b. 1892)
  - Otto Klemperer, German-born conductor (b. 1885)
- July 7
  - Max Horkheimer, German philosopher and sociologist (b. 1895)
  - Veronica Lake, American actress (b. 1922)
- July 8
  - Arthur Calwell, Australian labor politician (b. 1896)
  - Ben-Zion Dinur, Russian-born Israeli educator, historian and politician (b. 1884)
  - Wilfred Rhodes, English cricketer (b. 1877)
- July 11
  - Alexander Mosolov, Russian composer (b. 1900)
  - Robert Ryan, American actor (b. 1909)
- July 12 – Lon Chaney, Jr., American actor (b. 1906)
- July 13 – Willy Fritsch, German actor (b. 1901)
- July 18 – Jack Hawkins, British actor (b. 1910)
- July 20
  - Bruce Lee, Chinese-American martial artist and actor (b. 1940)
  - Robert Smithson, American artist (b. 1938)
- July 23 – Eddie Rickenbacker, American World War I flying ace and race car driver (b. 1890)
- July 25
  - Amy Jacques Garvey, Jamaican-born journalist and activist (b. 1895)
  - Louis St. Laurent, 12th Prime Minister of Canada (b. 1882)
- July 29
  - Henri Charrière, French writer (b. 1906)

- Roger Williamson, British race car driver (b. 1948)

August

Walter Ulbricht

Karl Ziegler

Fulgencio Batista

- August 1
  - Gian Francesco Malipiero, Italian composer (b. 1882)
  - Walter Ulbricht, East German leader (b. 1893)
- August 2 – Jean-Pierre Melville, French film director (b. 1917)
- August 4 – Eddie Condon, American jazz musician (b. 1905)
- August 6
  - Fulgencio Batista, Cuban dictator (b. 1901)

- o James Beck, British actor (b. 1929)
- August 9 – Charles Daniels, American Olympic swimmer (b. 1885)
- August 10 – Douglas Kennedy, American actor (b. 1915)
- August 11 – Karl Ziegler, German chemist, Nobel Prize laureate (b. 1898)
- August 12
  - o Dayanand Bandodkar, Chief Minister of Goa (b. 1911)
  - o Walter Rudolf Hess, Swiss physiologist, Nobel Prize laureate (b. 1881)
- August 13 – Willy Rey, American model (b. 1949)
- August 16
  - o Veda Ann Borg, American actress (b. 1915)
  - o Selman Waksman, Ukrainian-born biochemist, recipient of the Nobel Prize in Physiology or Medicine (b. 1888)
- August 17
  - o Conrad Aiken, American writer (b. 1889)
  - o Jean Barraqué, French composer (b. 1928)
  - o Paul Williams, American singer (The Temptations) (b. 1939)
- August 27 – Tol Avery, American actor (b. 1915)
- August 30 – Michael Dunn, American actor (b. 1934)
- August 31 – John Ford, American film director (b. 1894)

September

J. R. R. Tolkien

Salvador Allende

Gustaf VI Adolf of Sweden

- September 2
  - ○ Diana Sands, American actress (b. 1934)
  - ○ J. R. R. Tolkien, British writer (b. 1892)
- September 11 – Salvador Allende, President of Chile (b. 1908)
- September 13
  - ○ Betty Field, American actress (b. 1913)
  - ○ Sajjad Zaheer, Urdu writer and revolutionary (b. 1905)
- September 15
  - ○ King Gustaf VI Adolf of Sweden (b. 1882)
  - ○ Víctor Jara, Chilean politician and singer-songwriter (b. 1932)
  - ○ Robert B. McClure, American general (b. 1896)
- September 18 – Ken Harada, first diplomat from Japan to the Holy See (age 80)
- September 19 – Gram Parsons, American musician (b. 1946)
- September 20
  - ○ Jim Croce, American songwriter (b. 1943)
  - ○ Glenn Strange, American actor (b. 1899)
- September 23 – Pablo Neruda, Chilean poet, Nobel Prize laureate (b. 1904)

- September 24 – Josué de Castro, Brazilian writer, physician, geographer and activist against hunger (b. 1908)
- September 26
  - Ralph Earnhardt, American race car driver (b. 1928)
  - Anna Magnani, Italian actress (b. 1908)
- September 28 – Norma Crane, American actress (b. 1928)
- September 29 – W. H. Auden, English poet (b. 1907)
- September 30 – Peter Pitseolak, Inuit photographer and author (b. 1902)

October

Paavo Nurmi

Pablo Casals

Abebe Bikila

- October 2
  - Paul Hartman, American dancer and actor (b. 1904)
  - Paavo Nurmi, Finnish runner (b. 1897)
- October 6
  - Sidney Blackmer, American actor (b. 1895)
  - François Cevert, French race car driver (b. 1944)
- October 8 – Gabriel Marcel, French Catholic existential thinker (b. 1889)
- October 10 – Ludwig von Mises, Austrian economist (b. 1881)
- October 14
  - Edmund A. Chester, American broadcaster and journalist (b. 1897)
  - Ahmed Hamdi, Egyptian general who fought in Yom Kippur (b. 1929)
- October 16 – Gene Krupa, American jazz drummer (b. 1909)
- October 17 – Ingeborg Bachmann, Austrian writer (b. 1926)
- October 18
  - Walt Kelly, American cartoonist (b. 1913)
  - Crane Wilbur, American actor (b. 1886)
- October 19 – Margaret Caroline Anderson, American magazine publisher (b. 1886)
- October 22 – Pablo Casals, Spanish cellist and conductor (b. 1876)
- October 25 – Abebe Bikila, Ethiopian long-distance runner (b. 1932)
- October 26 Semyon Budyonny, Cossack cavalryman and Marshal of the Soviet Union (b. 1883)
- October 27 – Allan "Rocky" Lane, American actor (b. 1909)

- October 28 – Cleo Moore, American actress (b. 1928)

November

- November 2 – Greasy Neale, American football coach (Philadelphia Eagles) and a member of the Pro Football Hall of Fame (b. 1891)
- November 3 – Marc Allégret, French film director (b. 1900)
- November 7 – Kiyohide Shima, Japanese admiral (b. 1890)
- November 9 – Apostol Karamitev, Bulgarian actor (b. 1923)
- November 10
  - David "Stringbean" Akeman, American banjo player (b. 1915)
  - Morton Deyo, American admiral (b. 1887)
- November 11 – Artturi Ilmari Virtanen, Finnish chemist, Nobel Prize laureate (b. 1895)
- November 13 – Lila Lee, American actress (b. 1901)
- November 16 – Alan Watts, British philosopher (b. 1915)
- November 20 – Allan Sherman, American comedy writer, television producer, and song parodist (b. 1924)
- November 23
  - Sessue Hayakawa, Japanese-American actor (b. 1889)
  - Constance Talmadge, American actress (b. 1897)
- November 25 – Laurence Harvey, English actor (b. 1928)
- November 27 – Frank Christian, American musician (b. 1887)
- November 28 – John Rostill, English bassist, musician and composer (The Shadows) (b. 1942)
- November 29 – Philip D. Gallery, American admiral (b. 1907)

December

David Ben-Gurion

Bobby Darin

Ismet Inonu

- December 1 – David Ben-Gurion, Prime Minister of Israel (b. 1886)
- December 2 – Richard G. Colbert, American admiral (b. 1915)
- December 3 – Emile Christian, American musician (b. 1895)
- December 4 – Michael O'Shea, American actor (b. 1906)
- December 5 – Sir Robert Watson-Watt, Scottish engineer, radar pioneer (b. 1892)
- December 20
  - Luis Carrero Blanco, first minister of Spain (assassinated) (b. 1904)
  - Bobby Darin, American singer, songwriter, musician, actor, dancer, impressionist and TV presenter (b. 1936)
- December 23 – Gerard Kuiper Netherlands-born American astronomer (b. 1905)
- December 24 – Fritz Gause, German historian (b. 1893)
- December 25
  - İsmet İnönü, Turkish general, later Prime Minister, President (b. 1884)

- o Adrian Scott, American screenwriter, one of the Hollywood Ten (b. 1912)
  - o Gabriel Voisin, French aviation pioneer (b. 1880)
- December 26
  - o William Haines, American actor (b. 1900)
  - o Harold B. Lee, American president of The Church of Jesus Christ of Latter-day Saints (b. 1899)
- December 30 – Marcel-Bruno Gensoul, French admiral (b. 1880)

Nobel Prizes

- Physics – Leo Esaki, Ivar Giaever, Brian David Josephson
- Chemistry – Ernst Otto Fischer, Geoffrey Wilkinson
- Medicine – Karl von Frisch, Konrad Lorenz, Nikolaas Tinbergen
- Literature – Patrick White
- Peace – Henry Kissinger, Lê Đức Thọ
- Economics – Wassily Leontief

In the News

Britain Ireland and Denmark join the EEC.

World Trade Center in New York becomes the tallest building in the world.

Watergate Hearings begin in the United States Senate and President Richard Nixon tells the nation , "I am not a crook."

Sydney Opera House is opened.

In a Tennis Match billed as the battle of the sexes Mrs Billy Jean King defeats Bobby Riggs.

Princess Anne, marries Captain Mark Phillips in Westminster Abbey.

Popular Films - The Exorcist, Deliverance, Live and Let Die.

Skylab, the United States' first space station, is launched.

The Sears Tower opens in Chicago.

In the UK, as a result of high coal and oil prices, the Three-Day Week officially comes into force.

US Troops withdrawn from Vietnam.

1973 Calendar

January 1973
Sun	Mon	Tue	Wed	Thu	Fri	Sat
	1	2	3	4	5	6
7	8	9	10	11	12	13
14	15	16	17	18	19	20
21	22	23	24	25	26	27
28	29	30	31			

February 1973
Sun	Mon	Tue	Wed	Thu	Fri	Sat
				1	2	3
4	5	6	7	8	9	10
11	12	13	14	15	16	17
18	19	20	21	22	23	24
25	26	27	28			

March 1973
Sun	Mon	Tue	Wed	Thu	Fri	Sat
				1	2	3
4	5	6	7	8	9	10
11	12	13	14	15	16	17
18	19	20	21	22	23	24
25	26	27	28	29	30	31

April 1973
Sun	Mon	Tue	Wed	Thu	Fri	Sat
1	2	3	4	5	6	7
8	9	10	11	12	13	14
15	16	17	18	19	20	21
22	23	24	25	26	27	28
29	30					

May 1973
Sun	Mon	Tue	Wed	Thu	Fri	Sat
		1	2	3	4	5
6	7	8	9	10	11	12
13	14	15	16	17	18	19
20	21	22	23	24	25	26
27	28	29	30	31		

June 1973
Sun	Mon	Tue	Wed	Thu	Fri	Sat
					1	2
3	4	5	6	7	8	9
10	11	12	13	14	15	16
17	18	19	20	21	22	23
24	25	26	27	28	29	30

July 1973
Sun	Mon	Tue	Wed	Thu	Fri	Sat
1	2	3	4	5	6	7
8	9	10	11	12	13	14
15	16	17	18	19	20	21
22	23	24	25	26	27	28
29	30	31				

August 1973
Sun	Mon	Tue	Wed	Thu	Fri	Sat
			1	2	3	4
5	6	7	8	9	10	11
12	13	14	15	16	17	18
19	20	21	22	23	24	25
26	27	28	29	30	31	

September 1973
Sun	Mon	Tue	Wed	Thu	Fri	Sat
						1
2	3	4	5	6	7	8
9	10	11	12	13	14	15
16	17	18	19	20	21	22
23	24	25	26	27	28	29
30						

October 1973
Sun	Mon	Tue	Wed	Thu	Fri	Sat
	1	2	3	4	5	6
7	8	9	10	11	12	13
14	15	16	17	18	19	20
21	22	23	24	25	26	27
28	29	30	31			

November 1973
Sun	Mon	Tue	Wed	Thu	Fri	Sat
				1	2	3
4	5	6	7	8	9	10
11	12	13	14	15	16	17
18	19	20	21	22	23	24
25	26	27	28	29	30	

December 1973
Sun	Mon	Tue	Wed	Thu	Fri	Sat
						1
2	3	4	5	6	7	8
9	10	11	12	13	14	15
16	17	18	19	20	21	22
23	24	25	26	27	28	29
30	31